T   S

The Vikings?
King Alfred   15
Living Together   19
   Living in the Country   20
   Building Towns   24
   New Words   28
   The Invaders Change   30
   Bede, the Busy Historian   32
   Sutton Hoo – A Discovery   33
   Vikings All Around   36
   Thinking Back
Glossary
Index

Introduction

In this book we are going to go back a long way in time to find out what Britain was like then and who came to live here. They are some of our **ancestors**, or relations from long ago. Some of them came peacefully but most of them were soldiers and raiders. They invaded and fought to gain some land. When they felt safe they settled down to farm and their families came to join them.

We have some ideas or **evidence** about what life was like then from things found by archaeologists, from towns and villages which they have dug up, from graves and from the few historians who were writing then.

A model of a Roman soldier.

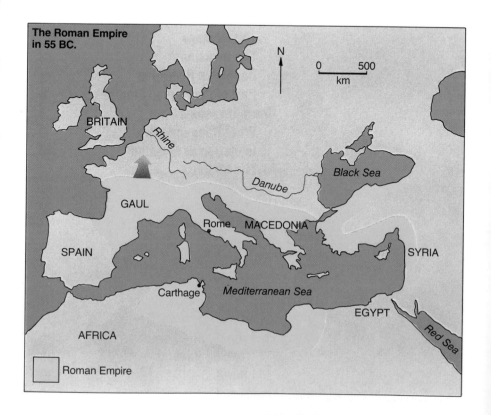

The Roman Empire in 55 BC.

N

0   500
km

BRITAIN

Rhine

GAUL

Danube

Black Sea

Rome   MACEDONIA

SPAIN

SYRIA

Carthage   Mediterranean Sea

EGYPT

Red Sea

AFRICA

Roman Empire

The Invasions

It was 55 BC. Trouble was coming. The Celtic people who lived in Britain had heard about it from the Celts in Gaul (France). Trouble was the great Roman army and its general, Julius Caesar.

Caesar had taken all of Gaul and now he wanted Britain. The first time Julius Caesar came the Celts attacked him with their chariots. He had to go back to Gaul. But the next year, 54 BC, he came back with an even bigger army.

This time he landed nearer London and was helped by some Celts who did not like their king. Caesar won the battle. He took some hostages and went back to Rome.

Over 90 years went by. The new Emperor Claudius wanted the silver and gold from the mines in Britain and the good farms. By now the Roman **Empire** was even bigger and the Roman army even stronger.

General Plautius and Emperor Claudius **invaded** Britain easily in AD 43. They had friends here already. They planned that the army would stay.

▲ A carving of Caesar's army.

ACTIVITIES

1 Why were the three invasions different? Why did the Romans stay the third time and not before?

2 We know about Julius Caesar because he wrote a diary. Do you think he would be fair to the Celts?

3 Look at the pictures of the Roman soldiers – what can you find out from them?

Boudica's Rebellion

The Romans built forts and had a big army. But the Celts did not give up. Some of them went to their high hill forts with deep ditches all around to be safe. They did not like being ruled by Romans. Queen Boudica led a large **rebellion** against the Romans.

Boudica was Queen of the Iceni tribe. Roman soldiers had robbed her and taken farms from the Celts.

Boudica called for all the Celtic tribesmen to help her. Lots of them came because they were so angry with the Romans. They wanted the Romans to leave Britain. They marched to Colchester. They captured it, burnt it and then did the same in London. They all moved on to St Albans and did the same there. Many people who got on well with the Romans were killed.

Boudica and her army marched on to fight the Roman general called Paulinus. They felt very brave.

▶ Maiden Castle – a Celtic fort.

The Roman army was smaller but it was well trained. Paulinus chose a good spot to fight. The Celts had no plan. They rushed at the Romans who threw javelins, and then used their swords. The Romans won and killed all the Celtic families who had come to watch.

We know about Boudica because of a Roman called Tacitus.

He wrote the life story of his father-in-law who was called Agricola. Agricola was in Paulinus' army and told Tacitus the story years later.

▲ The helmet of a Roman soldier.

▲ A Roman dagger.

ACTIVITIES

1 Why do we not have the Celtic side to the Boudica story? Can you write it now as if you were a Celtic tribesman? Look at the story carefully.

2 Do you think that Boudica was wise to start a rebellion?

Part of the Roman Empire

After Boudica's rebellion, the Romans had no more real trouble. They built Hadrian's Wall in about AD 120 to keep out the Picts in the north. The Romans settled down to build towns and farms.

In the country the big houses with farms were called villas. The Roman family lived on one side of the house and the rest was for stores, the kitchen and the slaves.

The Romans wanted Britain to be like the rest of their empire. They built big houses with under-floor heating. They painted pictures on the walls and put mosaics on the floor.

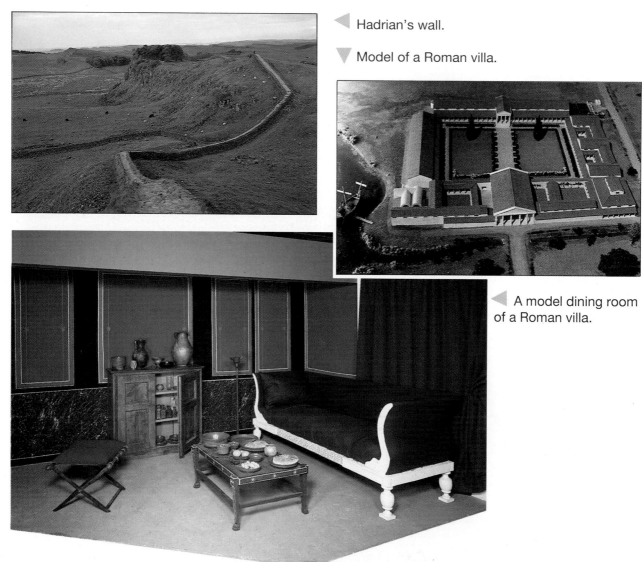

◀ Hadrian's wall.

▼ Model of a Roman villa.

◀ A model dining room of a Roman villa.

Ploughing the land.

The army needed food, leather and wool. The villa farms grew corn. Animals like sheep and cattle were kept. In some places the Romans made iron tools and weapons. They were sold to the army or in the markets.

Some of the things made in Britain went by boat to be sold in Gaul or Rome. Wine and oil came back to Britain in these boats.

The Romans planned and built towns with a market place. They had water pipes and drain pipes. They built temples for their gods, like Jupiter, king of the gods. Nearby they sometimes built baths and an **amphitheatre.**

The Roman baths at Bath.

Often the girls and boys went to school – but they had to pay. They wrote on slabs of wax with a sharp stick. They learnt Latin and wore Roman clothes.

▲ Roman writing tablet.

▲ Emerald and gold necklace.

Many of the Celts learnt to be skilled workers, making tools, weapons, pots and jewellery.

Soon the Celts could not remember what it had been like before the Romans came.

Why did they go?

The Romans came in AD 43. By AD 412 they had gone.

There were many attacks by tribes outside the Roman Empire. The Emperor called more and more soldiers back from Britain to help with the fighting. The Picts kept breaking through Hadrian's Wall and the Roman soldiers had to push them back. This happened again and again.

More and more Roman soldiers left Britain until one day they had all gone.

ACTIVITIES

1 With a friend choose one of the things the Romans did and find out more about it to tell the rest of the class.

2 Mosaics are pictures or patterns made up of tiny pieces of tile. Find pictures of them. Can you design a floor like the Romans? How will you do it?

More Invasions

What Happened Next?

The grand rooms of the villas were empty. The Roman Governor and his family had gone with the soldiers. Now, who would catch the robbers on the roads? Who would now buy all the food grown for the army?

The people asked their village leader. He said they must look after themselves. Soon villages joined into groups and chose a leader. Everyone felt safer that way. People left the Roman towns. The farmers just grew food for their own families. They wanted to be left in peace.

There was no peace. The Picts and Scots and Anglo-Saxon pirates came **raiding**. The Celts were led by a man called Vortigern. They did not fight as an army. They did not win. Vortigern looked about for help.

A fort which the Roman soldiers left behind in Porchester.

Invitation or Invasion?

Vortigern asked the Angles and the Saxons to help.

Bede, a **monk** who wrote a history of England many years later, wrote,

. . . In AD 449 the Angles or Saxons came to Britain in three longships. They were invited by Vortigern and were given lands in return for protecting the country . . . but their real plan was to rule it.

. . . These pagan invaders ruined the towns and the countryside . . . and ruled this sad island. Buildings, priests and people were burnt and killed . . . A few miserable people hid in the hills. They starved and had to give themselves up to be slaves, or be killed. Some lived a fearful life among the mountains . . . always on the watch for danger.

Jutes

Angles

Saxons

Britain

Fresians

N

0   500
km

The Anglo-Saxons came from tribes of Angles, Saxons and Jutes.

Some of the Celts went back to live in the hill forts where hundreds of years before, they had hidden from the Romans.

The Romans had ruled for about 400 years. They had gone by AD 412. The Anglo-Saxons arrived soon after. There were battles between the Anglo-Saxons and the Celts to start with. But slowly the Anglo-Saxons took over and made their own small kingdoms.

An Anglo-Saxon helmet.

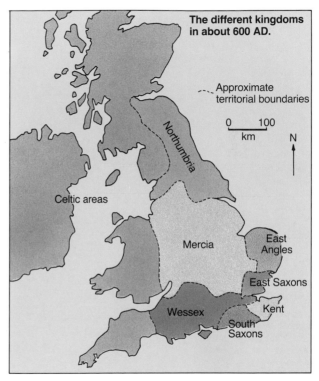

The different kingdoms in about 600 AD.

Approximate territorial boundaries

0   100
km

N

Northumbria

Celtic areas

Mercia

East Angles

East Saxons

Wessex

Kent

South Saxons

ACTIVITIES

1 How do you think we know the people left the Roman towns?

2 Was the coming of the Anglo-Saxons an **invasion** or an invitation?

3 Bede wrote his history in AD 731. How many years later was this? How do you think he knew about events which happened so long ago? Can you be sure that what he writes is true?

The Vikings!

The different Anglo-Saxon kings had battles, but often they all lived together in peace. Suddenly, this all changed. The monks wrote about it in their records, called the Anglo-Saxon **Chronicles**;

In this year, AD 793, terrible signs appeared which . . . frightened the inhabitants; there were flashes of lightning, and fiery dragons were seen flying through the air. A great famine followed these signs . . . On 8th June the Vikings violently destroyed God's church of Lindisfarne.

Here is another story from the chronicles;

While Brihtric was king over Wessex [AD 788 – 802] . . . three fast Viking ships came unexpectedly . . . and this was their first coming . . . Beaduheard, the king's servant, leapt on his horse and with a few men galloped to the port. He thought they were merchants not enemies . . . He ordered them to be taken to the king. But he and his men were killed by them.

The prow of a ship.

The Vikings had some new technology. They had invented the fastest, strongest long ships. They used these ships to make surprise attacks. At night they rowed silently up a river and in the morning they robbed homes, churches and monasteries. They always came in the summer and did not stay long.

After AD 851, the Vikings began to live in Kent all year round. Then they **conquered** East Anglia and killed the king. They took the farms from the Anglo-Saxons and made the Anglo-Saxons work with them. The Vikings took York and called it Jorvik. Some Vikings became **traders**.

▼ A Viking ship which was re-built from evidence by archaeologists.

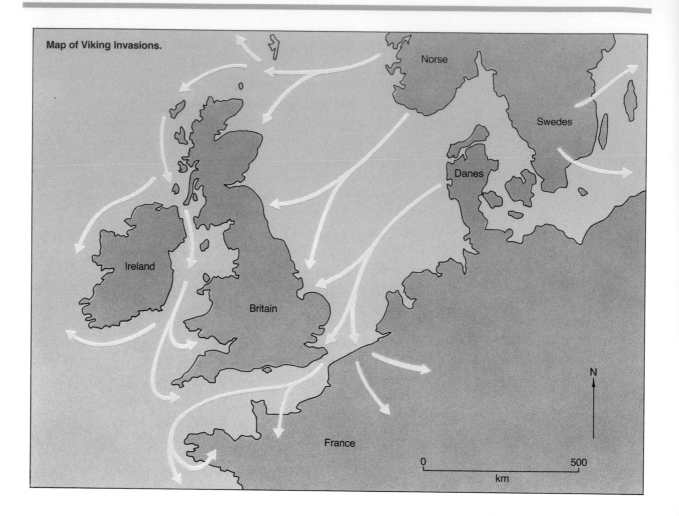

Map of Viking Invasions.

Norse

Swedes

Danes

Ireland

Britain

France

N

0   500
km

ACTIVITIES

1 Do we know which Viking raid was the first? Can we be sure?

2 The Chronicles were written by **Christian monks** who lived and prayed in **monasteries**. The Vikings were **pagans**. Look up in the glossary to find out what these words mean. Do you think the monks would be fair to the Vikings in their writings?

3 Look at the second story from the Chronicles. Can you act out the story? Pretend to be one of the Vikings and write a letter home saying what happened.

4 Compare the two stories on page 12. What were the Vikings like?

King Alfred

In 871 Alfred became king of Wessex. The first thing he had to do was to go on fighting the Vikings.

The Vikings made the Anglo-Saxons pay Danegeld silver to them. If they paid the Vikings left them in peace. If they did not pay the Vikings attacked them. Alfred did not want to pay this money. He led the other Anglo-Saxon kings in their fight against the Vikings.

In 877 Alfred sent his soldiers home for Christmas but the Vikings made a surprise attack against him. Alfred escaped with some friends. They were in great danger. They went down secret tracks in the marshlands which the Vikings did not know about.

▲ An Anglo-Saxon sword.

The next Spring, Alfred and his soldiers attacked the Viking leader, Guthrum, and won. Alfred and Guthrum made peace. They shared England between them. Guthrum's part was called Danelaw.

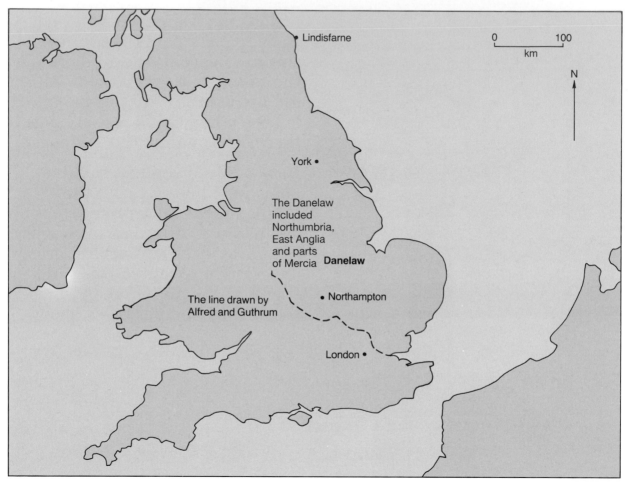

Lindisfarne

0   100
km

N

York •

The Danelaw
included
Northumbria,
East Anglia
and parts
of Mercia   **Danelaw**

The line drawn by
Alfred and Guthrum

• Northampton

London •

Making Wessex Safe

Alfred wanted Wessex to be safe if the Vikings did attack again. He made sure that there were always men ready to fight. They took it in turns to be in the army and to be at home looking after their farms. He also made the navy stronger.

Alfred had many more ideas about things he wanted to do once there was peace.

Alfred also looked for some big villages to make into towns called burhs with strong walls where people could go if the Vikings came. Some became big market towns.

In Peace

There were different laws in different areas and people did not understand them. Alfred made one set of laws for everyone and wrote them in English. He called all his wise men to a meeting called the Witan to ask them if they thought the laws were fair. Alfred wrote:

> Then I showed the laws to all my councillors, and they then said that they were pleased to obey them.

Alfred wanted the monks to learn to read and write Latin. One monk called Asser became his friend and wrote a book all about King Alfred.

While Alfred was king all the records from the monasteries were translated into English. Copies were sent to monks and they were told to go on with the records. These records are called The Anglo-Saxon **Chronicles** and they tell the history of Britain.

▼ The Alfred Jewel. It says, 'Alfred had me made.'

Alfred was a Christian. He had been to visit the Pope in Rome twice before he was nine years old. He wanted everyone to be Christian. He sent a book by Pope Gregory to all the bishops, telling them how to help the people love Jesus.

Alfred persuaded Guthrum and some of his Viking friends to become Christians too.

Coin of King Alfred.

After Alfred

For nearly two hundred years, the Vikings and the Anglo-Saxons lived together. Sometimes the kings had battles. Little by little, the small kingdoms joined together to make one big kingdom. Sometimes it was ruled by a Viking and sometimes by an Anglo-Saxon.

There was one last invasion of Britain. William of Normandy, who came from a Viking family, invaded in 1066 with his Norman army. But that is another story . . .

ACTIVITIES

1 Would Alfred remember the first Viking raids?

2 The monks wrote about Alfred as a great and good king. Why do you think this was? How many reasons can you find?

3 Can you make your own school chronicle?

Living Together

The Anglo-Saxons began invading Britain about 300 years before the Vikings started raiding and then invading. Here is a list of what the two groups had in common.

1 They both came from lands across the sea from Britain.
2 They both built their houses of wood and thatch.
3 They both wore the same sort of clothes.
4 They wrote in the same way.
5 They shared the same gods and then became Christians.
6 They invaded Britain for some of the same reasons.
7 The men all liked to follow a brave leader.
8 They used the same kinds of weapons.
9 They listened to the same sagas.

They lived in Britain together for over 200 years. It is very difficult to separate them so we are going to learn about them together.

Below right: A model Viking town built by archaeologists at the Jorvik museum in York.
Below left: The Anglo-Saxon village at West Stow has been re-built, people are dressed up like Anglo-Saxons.

ACTIVITIES

1 If they were so alike why did they fight each other? Think back to the story of the invasions and make a list.

Living in the Country

The Invaders came because there were too many people in their own countries. A family needed a farm and there was not enough farm-land to go round. The men became pirates and raiders to get treasure. Some of them joined an invading army. When they had some land and felt safe their family came over to live with them. Other families moved to Britain because they heard about the good land for farming.

When they came to Britain they got land in different ways. Sometimes they fought the people here, but sometimes people ran away and left their farms empty. Some people may have been made slaves of the new **settlers**, especially if they tried to fight. Others may have been allowed to stay or even marry into the new families.

▼ This is what a farmer would have used to plough his fields. It would have been pulled by oxen.

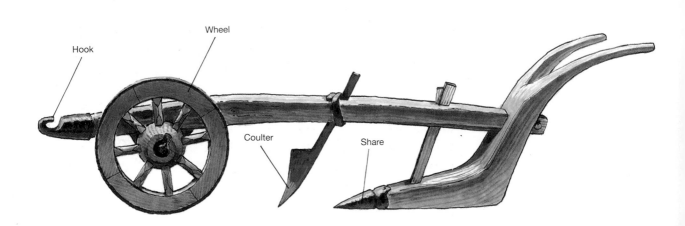

Hook

Wheel

Coulter

Share

As more people came more houses and villages had to be built. Houses were made out of wood. We can learn about them from the work of **archaeologists**.

Archaeologists found the site where there was an Anglo-Saxon village at West Stow. They found pits and post holes in the ground, like those in the picture.

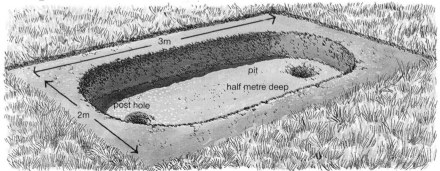

With this **evidence** they thought that the Anglo-Saxon houses looked like this.

▶ The family lived on the pit floor.

But the archaeologists found more clues because two houses had burnt down. The burned wood which was left gave the archaeologists more important evidence. They now think the houses looked like this:

▶ One of the Anglo-Saxon houses made by the archaeologists. There are wooden floors over the pit.

The archeologists began to re-build part of the Anglo-Saxon village from the evidence they found.

It is a copy of part of the village that was there until about AD 650. The houses are in a group with a bigger hall in the middle. They may have shared their meals there together and had meetings.

West Stow about 650 AD

High dry land – sheep grazing

Trade:
Out – grain, wool, hides.
In – metalwork, seashells, glass.

clay pit

Woodland – hunting, timber, pigs, etc.

Crops: wheat, barley, rye, peas, etc.

cemetery

Line of old Roman road

ford

Meadows cattle

cattle

Icknield Way

River: – Water, birds, fish, transport.

ford

We know that they kept cows and sheep near the village. They grew crops in the fields. Pigs, hens and geese were kept. The bones of cats and dogs were also found near the village. There were many different jobs to do in the village.

▶ The blacksmith at West Stow.

The Invaders had warm wooden houses with a **thatched** roof, a wooden floor and a fire on a clay hearth. In the corner was a bed with skins and woollen blankets. There were benches round the wall near the fire, some stools and a table. The pit under the planks helped to keep the floor dry and the thatch kept the house warm. Now some people go to West Stow. They dress up and do the same sorts of jobs that the Anglo-Saxons did.

▼Spinning and dyeing at West Stow.

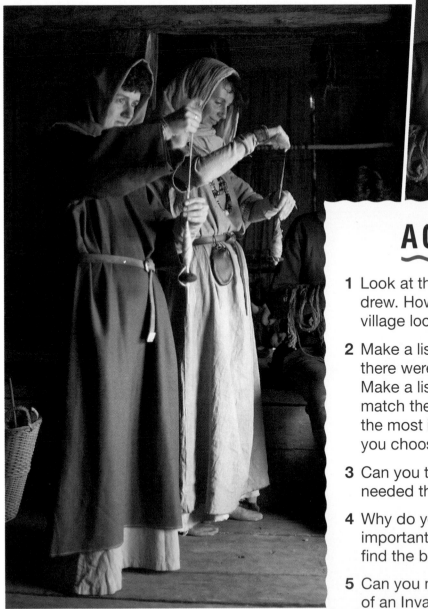

ACTIVITIES

1 Look at the map the archaeologists drew. How did they know what the village looked like?

2 Make a list of all the jobs you think there were to do in the village. Make a list of a big family and then match the jobs. Which jobs were the most important? Which would you choose?

3 Can you think of anything they needed that they did not make?

4 Why do you think it was so important for the archaeologists to find the burned wood?

5 Can you make a model of the home of an Invader?

Building Towns

Some of the Invaders did not come to Britain to be a farming family and stay in a village. Some of them wanted to make things to sell.

Little by little the old Roman market towns grew again. People used the tumble-down Roman walls to make part of a new house. Other towns grew from villages and the houses were made of wood and thatch.

They did not always clear the mud from the road or mend the drains. The people in the towns grew some fruit and vegetables in their gardens. They needed to buy more meat, corn and salt. The markets grew and the towns grew.

Trade

▼ A model ship bringing things into Britain at the Jorvik museum.

Britain sold cloth, pottery and slaves to countries across the sea. Britain could not make good wine so that came back in the ships, together with furs.

Living in Towns

The town we know most about is Jorvik (now called York). The Romans had built a town there and so had the Anglo-Saxons. The Vikings captured it and changed its name to Jorvik. They made it the capital of the Danelaw. It became very rich and important.

Just like West Stow we know about it from the archaeologists. Archaeologists began digging in York. They found a lot of **evidence** about life in the town. Houses and streets have been built to show people what life was like for the Invaders in Jorvik.

▼ Archaeologists had to dig down to find Viking remains.

The houses were just like farmhouses but they started lower down. Here the floor was nearly 2 metres below ground level. A wide hole was dug and the wooden house was built. Some of the walls and the roof were above the ground. Stone steps led down to the door. The front was a workshop for making and selling things.

▶ The jeweller at the Jorvik museum.

Making things

Making coins was one of the most important jobs. There was no paper money. The kings said who could make coins. The biggest mints were in London, Canterbury and Jorvik but many other towns had them too.

Many things were made and sold in the towns. At the front of the house, in the light, people made things to sell. At the back, the houses were just like farm houses.

Wool was spun and then woven into cloth, or sometimes knitted into socks.

▼ A Viking sock the archaeologists found.

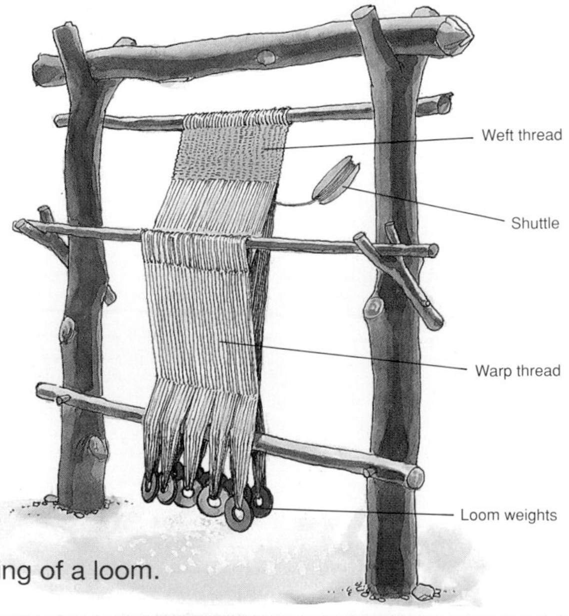

Weft thread

Shuttle

Warp thread

Loom weights

A drawing of a loom.

Viking silver.

Iron workers made helmets. They also made tools, knives, keys, weights and fish hooks.

The leather workers made shoes, bags and belts.
The coopers made wooden bowls, mugs, spoons and buckets.

Some of the Invaders came to find gold, silver and tin in the mines in Cornwall and Wales. They made beads, brooches, buckles and pins to sell.

Amber jewellery.

▲ Helmet found at Jorvik. It was made of iron with brass decorations in about AD 750.

ACTIVITIES

1 Look at the pictures of Roman villas. What is the same and what is different from the homes of the Anglo-Saxons and Vikings?

2 Why did the kings always want to say who could make coins?

3 Why did they use antlers and not plastic to make combs?

4 Make a list of all the things you think the archaeologists found in Jorvik. Use the pictures and the writing.

5 Why did they always need salt?

New Words

When the Anglo-Saxons and later the Vikings came, they had their own gods. There were many **sagas** or stories about Odin, the father god, Freya, the goddess of love and Thor, Odin's eldest son.

Thor had a chariot drawn by goats, a hammer that could kill giants and break rocks. He wore a belt which doubled his strength and iron gloves to hold the hammer.

Slowly the people of Britain and the Invaders made just one language. Later it was called English. Here are some of the words they gave us.

Our word		Invaders' word
Monday day of the moon.		**Mondandaeg**
Tuesday day of Tiw – god of war and the sky.		**Tiwesdaeg**
Wednesday day of Woden – god of wisdom, war and poetry.		**Wodnesdaeg**
Thursday day of Thunor – god of thunder, sky and weather.		**Thunresdaeg**
Friday day of Frig – goddess of love and growing things.		**Frigesdaeg**

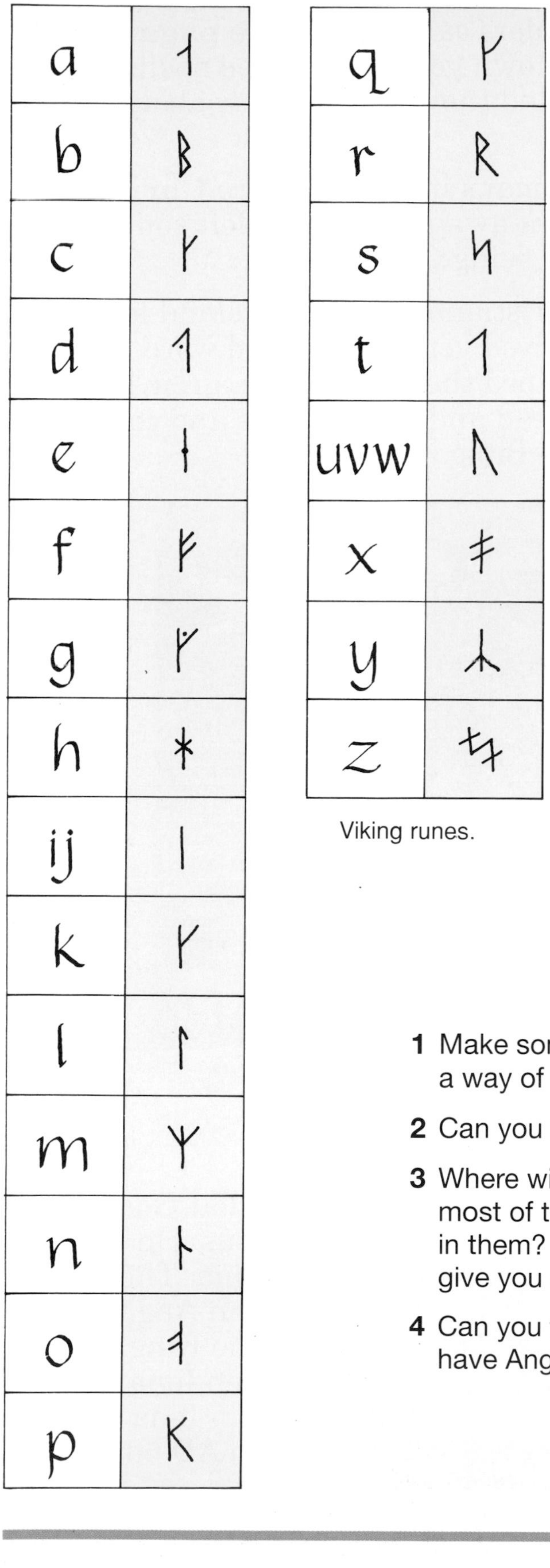
a
b
c
d
e
f
g
h
ij
k
l
m
n
o
p
q
r
s
t
uvw
x
y
z

Viking runes.

The Anglo-Saxons gave us these words: have, be, do, go, and, but.

The Vikings gave us these words: bread, eggs, cake, happy, angry, ugly, sky, ill, wrong, low, die.

Both the Anglo-Saxons and the Vikings gave places new names.

Anglo-Saxon place names often had 'ing' in them. They also often ended in 'ton' or 'ham'.

Viking words which were part of place names include 'thorpe' meaning village, 'thwaite' meaning paddock, 'by' meaning town and 'kirk' meaning church.

At first the Invaders carved letters called runes on stone, wood or bits of pottery. They did not write on paper. They wrote short messages and kept stories in their heads.

ACTIVITIES

1 Make some clay or plasticine tiles. Can you design a way of carving runes?

2 Can you find out about Saturday and Sunday?

3 Where will you look on a big map of England for most of the places with 'thorpe', 'thwaite', and 'by' in them? Look back in this book at the maps to give you a clue.

4 Can you find any places near where you live which have Anglo-Saxon or Viking names?

The Invaders Change

When the Invaders came they were **pagans**. They had their own gods. They used spells and lucky charms and they did not know about Jesus Christ.

Some of the Romans in Britain were **Christians** before they went away. After they left some people went on being Christian.

There were Christian **monks** in Ireland led by St Patrick. They lived very simply and wore no shoes. They helped the poor people, grew food and prayed. They read and wrote books and copied out parts of the Bible.

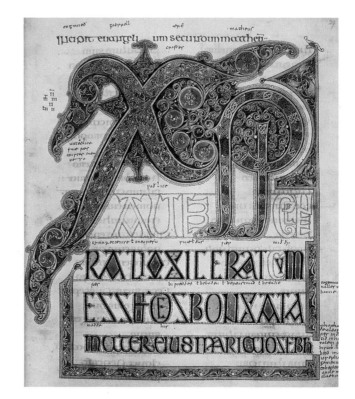

A page from the Lindisfarne gospels (part of the Bible copied by the monks).

A Christian monument showing the three wise men.

St Columba was a monk who said that God wanted him to tell others about Jesus. He went to Scotland, to a small island called Iona. The king of Iona became a Christian. Later, an Anglo-Saxon invader called Oswald became King of Northumbria. He had been to stay on Iona. He invited St Aidan and the monks from Iona to set up a **monastery** in his kingdom. In AD 635 a monastery on Lindisfarne was built.

The **Pope** in Rome sent St Augustine to Britain in AD 597. His job was to make everyone Christian. He landed in Kent where Queen Bertha was already a Christian. The news of Jesus spread and more of the Invaders became Christian. Slowly, Britain became a Christian country, following the Pope in Rome.

The Invaders lived in wooden houses but they began to build the monasteries and churches of stone. Sometimes they had to move very big corner stones over fifty miles from the quarry to the new church. Some of our churches still have parts that were built by the Invaders.

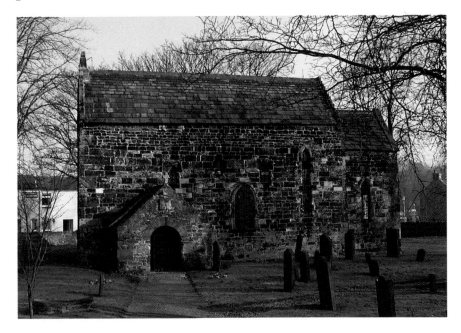

A Saxon church in County Durham, built about AD 800.

ACTIVITIES

1 How does a person become a Christian?

2 How do you think they moved the heavy corner stones?

3 Can you find out about St Patrick or St Augustine? Did they have the same ideas?

Bede, the Busy Historian

This is a story of a famous monk. He is famous because he wrote a very important book. Not many people wrote books then. When the Vikings raided many books were burnt. Bede's book was saved.

When he was a boy Bede lived in Northumbria and then he went to be a monk. He lived in the monastery most of his life. Like the other monks he went to pray nine times each day. They started very early. Each day the first prayers were at two o'clock in the morning. Bede was a teacher. He learnt about the Bible, the stars and how to be a doctor.

Bede looked for old records and books about Britain. He read lots of them. They did not all agree. Bede had to choose what to put in his book about the history of Britain.

▶ A picture of Bede writing his history.

ACTIVITIES

1 Do you think that Bede always knew what had happened?
Do you think he would be fair?

2 Why do you think there were so few books then?
Why are there more now?

Sutton Hoo

King Raedwald was an Anglo-Saxon king of East Anglia. He was very brave and many men wanted to fight for him. We know about him because a grave was found at Sutton Hoo in Suffolk, near the sea. Archaeologists think it was his grave.

▶ Archaeologists found a pattern of stains in the ground where the wood had rotted away.

King Raedwald died in about AD 625. He was put in a boat which his men had dragged up from the river. In it there were lots of treasures. They put a mound of earth on top to bury the king.

◀ The helmet as it would have looked when King Raedwald was alive. The pictures show Anglo-Saxon gods and fighters in battle. It was made of iron in about AD 625.

▼ A purse lid decorated with jewels.

▲ A dragon which decorated the shield.

A coin showing a cross. It was made between 605 and 615 in France.

The treasures were all the things the king would need in his next life. The Anglo-Saxons believed that dead people needed their things with them to use in the next life. Bede wrote that Raedwald was christened but Christians do not think that people need things in heaven. Did Raedwald ask for the treasures or did his friends put them in his grave for him?

Spoons which say 'Saul' and 'Paul'. They were often given as a Christening present.

ACTIVITIES

1 Look carefully at the helmet on the opposite page and the one from Jorvik on page 27. Make a list of all the things that are the same about them. Make a list of all the things that are different.

2 How do you think we know when the things were buried?

3 Look at the treasures. Pick one and see if you can copy it. What will you use?

4 Can you find out why the spoons had Saul and Paul on them?

5 Do you think that Raedwald was a Christian? How will you make up your mind?

Vikings All Around

The Anglo-Saxons wanted to get some land, to settle down and to farm. Some of the Vikings were the same but some wanted to be pirates or adventurers for ever.

These adventurers sailed up rivers into Russia looking for trade. Sometimes they carried their boats overland and they sailed down a river and across the Black Sea to Constantinople which was a great city.

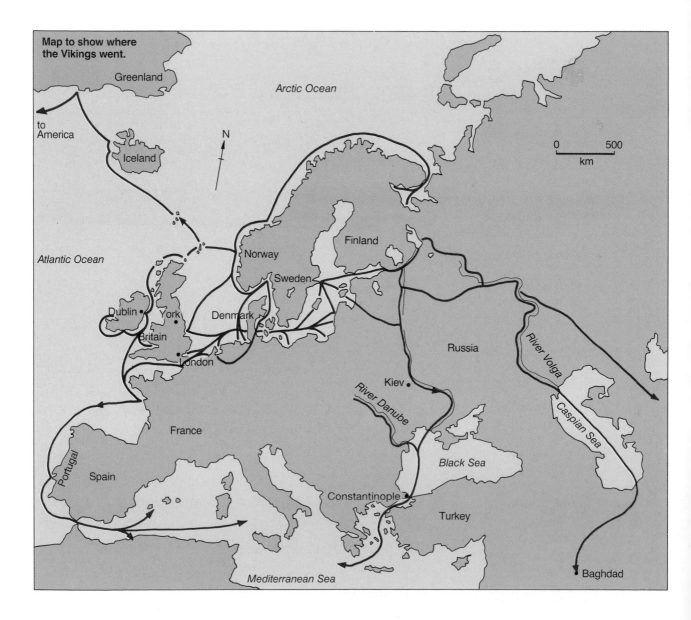

Map to show where the Vikings went.

A big army set out from Denmark and it never went home. It had well over 100 long ships. Sometimes this army attacked France and when that got too hard they attacked Britain. Then they would go back to France and Britain would be safe for a time. The king of France built a fleet and some forts, just like Alfred.

Vikings settled in Normandy, in Northern France. They also visited Italy, Spain, Morocco and Egypt.

Sometimes they just wanted to raid, sometimes they wanted land from the king and at other times they wanted to rule.

They went to Iceland and then to Greenland. It was warmer there then and they had farms. They sailed on to a place they called Vinland in their sagas. Many people think that Vinland was the Viking name for North America.

▶ A Viking ship found in Norway.

ACTIVITIES

1 What evidence do you think the Vikings left in all these places so that we know they were there?

Thinking Back

In this book we have read about three lots of people who invaded Britain at different times. They left different proofs and evidence that have been found in Britain.

ACTIVITIES

1 Think about the Romans, Anglo-Saxons and Vikings. Why did they become invaders and settlers? Which one would you have wanted to be?

2 Make a list of all the different sorts of evidence that tell us about these people. Which sort is the most helpful?

3 Make a plan to invite some visitors into your classroom. You must prove to them that the Anglo-Saxons or the Vikings did come to Britain. How will you do it?

4 What sort of evidence is your favourite? Which sort would you like to discover by yourself? Where would you look?

Glossary

amphitheatre Roman open air theatre where people went to see fighting and chariot races.

ancestor A relative from long ago.

archaeologist Someone who learns about the past, usually by digging things up.

Christian Someone who believes in the Christian religion, following the teachings of Jesus Christ.

chronicle List of what happened each year.

conquer To defeat and take control.

empire A group of countries ruled by one person or government.

evidence Something left from the past – includes writing, buildings, art, objects. If we look at them carefully they can give us proof about the past.

invade To enter with an army.

monastery A place where monks live and work.

monks Men who live in a religious group in a monastery.

pagan Someone who believes in lots of gods and not in one of the main religions.

Pope Head of the Catholic Christian Church.

raid A sudden attack.

rebellion When people fight against their rulers.

sagas Long stories about a hero's adventures.

settler A person who goes to live in a new country.

thatch Straw or reeds used to make a roof.

traders People who buy and sell things.

Index

Alfred, King   15-18
amphitheatre   7
Anglo-Saxon Chronicles   12, 17
Anglo-Saxon kingdoms   11, 18
archaeologists   2, 21, 22, 25, 33

baths, Roman   7
Bede   10, 32
Bertha, Queen   31
Boudica, Queen   4-5

Ceasar, Julius   3
Christianity   18, 19, 30-31
churches   31
Claudius, Emperor   3
clothes   19
coins   26
Colchester   4
craft, Anglo-Saxon   34-35
craft, Roman   8
craft, Viking   26, 27

Danegeld   15
Danelaw   16, 25

farms, Anglo-Saxon   20-22
farms, Roman   7

Gaul   3
gods, pagan   28, 30
graves   2, 33-35
Guthrum   16,18

Hadrian's Wall   6, 8
houses, town   24, 25
houses, village   19, 20-23

Icenii   4

Jorvik (York)   13, 24-27

laws, of Alfred   17
London   4

monasteries   30-31
monks   10, 12, 17, 30
mosaics   6

navy, Anglo-Saxon   16

Oswald, King   30

Paulinus, General   4, 5
Picts   8, 9
place names   29
Plautius, General   3
plough   20
Pope, the   18, 31

Raedwald, King   33-35
runes   29

sagas   28
St Aidan   30
St Albans   4
St Augustine   31
St Columba   30
St Patrick   30
school   8
ships, Viking   12, 13, 37

Tacitus   5
temples   7
towns, Anglo-Saxon   16
towns, Roman   7
towns, Viking   24-27
trade, Roman   7
trade, Viking   24

Viking journeys   36, 37
villages, Anglo-Saxon   20-23
villages, Roman   6, 9

weaving   26
West Stow   21-23
William of Normandy   18
Witan   17
words   28-29

Acknowledgements

The publisher would like to thank the following for permission to reproduce material.

Ancient Art and Architecture Collection p27 (bottom), p31. Ashmolean Museum p15, p17. British Museum p12, p17, p18, p26 (top), p30 (right), p32, p33 (both), p34 (both), p35 (both). CM Dixon p3, p6 (top left), p7 (bottom), p9. English Heritage p2, p4. Fishbourne Roman Palace p6 (top right). Jorvik Viking Centre, York Archaeological Trust p19, p24 (both), p25 (both), p26 (bottom), p27 (top and middle). The Manx Museum p13. Museum of London p5 (both), p6 (bottom), p7 (top), p8 (left). Universitets Olksaksamling p30 (right). Universitet I Oslo p34. West Stow Country Park p19, p21 (both), p22, p23.

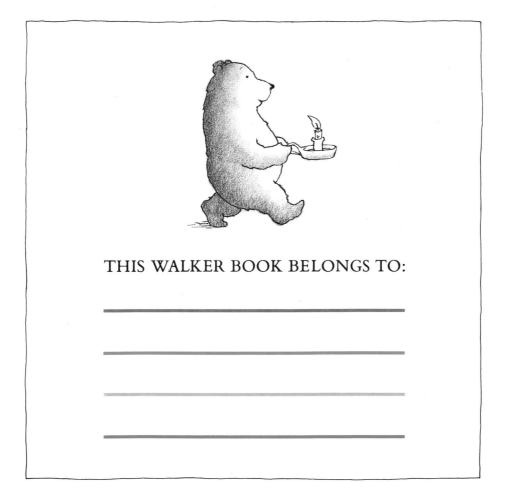

THIS WALKER BOOK BELONGS TO:

_____

_____

_____

_____

For Naomi

First published 1987 by Walker Books Ltd
87 Vauxhall Walk, London SE11 5HJ

This edition published 1988

© 1987 Blackbird Design Pty Ltd

Printed in Spain by Cayfosa, Barcelona

British Library Cataloguing in Publication Data
Graham, Bob
The red woollen blanket.
I. Title
741   PZ7
ISBN 0-7445-1132-1

THE RED WOOLLEN
BLANKET

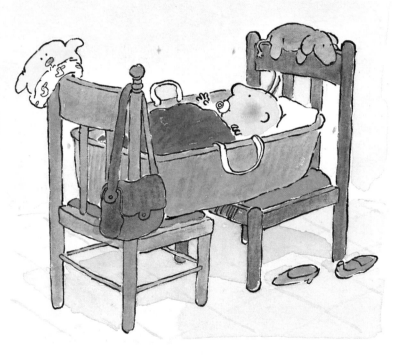

Bob Graham

WALKER BOOKS
LONDON

Julia had her own blanket right from the start.

Julia was born in the winter. She slept in her special cot wrapped tight as a parcel.
She had a band of plastic on her wrist with her name on it.

"She's as bald as an egg," said her father,
helping himself to another chocolate.

Julia came home from the hospital with her new red blanket, a bear, a grey woollen dog and a plastic duck.

Waiting at home for her were...

a large pair of pants with pink flowers and a beautiful
blue jacket specially knitted by her grandmother.

"Isn't blue for boys?"
"No, it doesn't really matter," said Mum.

Wrapped up in the red woollen blanket, Julia
slept in her own basket...

or in the front garden in the watery winter sunshine.

Her hair sprouted from the holes in her tea-cosy hat.
She smiled – nothing worried Julia.

Julia grew. She slept in a cot and sucked and chewed
the corners of her not-so-new blanket.

She rubbed the red woollen blanket gently against her nose.

Julia's mum carried her to the shops in a pack on her back. The pack was meant to carry the shopping.

Julia liked it so much up there that the pushchair was used for the shopping and the pack was used for Julia.

Then Julia was crawling and her blanket went with her.

It was chewed…

and screwed…

and oiled.

Some of it was left behind,

some went up the vacuum cleaner,

and some of it was trodden underfoot.

Then Julia took her first step.

Julia made her own small room from the blanket.
It was pink twilight under there.

From outside, the "creature" had a mind of its own.
It heaved and throbbed.

Wherever Julia went her blanket went too.

In the spring,

the summer,

the autumn,

and the winter.

Julia was getting bigger. Her blanket was getting smaller.
A sizeable piece was lost under the lawnmower.

"If Julia ran off deep into a forest," said her father, "she could find her way back by the blanket threads left behind."

The day that Julia started school,

she had a handy little blanket not much bigger than
a postage stamp –

because it would never do to take a whole blanket to school...

unless you were Billy, who used his blanket
as a "Lone Avenger's" cape.

Sometime during Julia's first day at school, she lost the last threads of her blanket.

It may have been while playing in the school yard...

or having her lunch under the trees.

It could have been anywhere at all...

and she hardly missed it.

MORE WALKER PAPERBACKS

FIRST READERS

Allan Ahlberg & Colin McNaughton
Red Nose Readers

MAKE A FACE   SO CAN I

BIG BAD PIG   BEAR'S BIRTHDAY

SHIRLEY'S SHOPS   PUSH THE DOG

TELL US A STORY   ONE, TWO, FLEA!

Colin West
'HAVE YOU SEEN THE CROCODILE?'

Colin & Jacqui Hawkins
TERRIBLE, TERRIBLE TIGER

Chris Riddell
BEN AND THE BEAR

Sarah Hayes & Helen Craig
THIS IS THE BEAR

PICTURE BOOKS
For 4 to 6-Year-Olds

Sarah Hayes
The Walker Fairy Tale Library
BOOKS ONE TO SIX
Six collections of favourite stories

Helen Craig
Susie and Alfred
THE NIGHT OF THE PAPER BAG MONSTERS

Philippe Dupasquier
ROBERT THE GREAT

Jane Asher & Gerald Scarfe
The Moppy Stories
MOPPY IS HAPPY   MOPPY IS ANGRY

PICTURE BOOKS
For 6 to 10-Year-Olds

Martin Waddell & Joseph Wright
Little Dracula

LITTLE DRACULA'S FIRST BITE

LITTLE DRACULA'S CHRISTMAS

LITTLE DRACULA AT THE SEASIDE

LITTLE DRACULA GOES TO SCHOOL

E.J. Taylor
Biscuit, Buttons and Pickles
IVY COTTAGE   GOOSE EGGS

Colin McNaughton
THE RAT RACE

Patrick Burston & Alastair Graham
Which Way?
THE PLANET OF TERROR
THE JUNGLE OF PERIL

David Lloyd & Charlotte Voake
THE RIDICULOUS STORY OF
GAMMER GURTON'S NEEDLE